Springer Spaniels

Illustrated by Jenny MacKendrick

First published 2015

The History Press
The Mill, Brimscombe Port
Stroud, Gloucestershire, GL5 2QG
www.thehistorypress.co.uk

British Library Cataloguing in Publication Data.
A catalogue record for this book is available from the
British Library.

ISBN 978 0 7509 6398 5

Design by The History Press
Printed in China

Springers ...

are dogs for all seasons.

They come in two different colours

and one length of tongue.

But they all have the same exuberant nature,

cheerful temperament

and desire to hunt

everything

and everybody.

Springers like ...

people ...

especially you!

They love to be praised,

run ...

and sniff.

There are smells everywhere!

They love to dig,

swim,

fetch

and get as muddy as possible

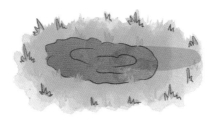

all at the same time.

They love licking

and balls.

And ... well, you guessed it.

Springers need ...

long walks

followed by long naps.

Lots of play ...

mostly with balls.

You can never have enough!

They need to be with you ...

or they'll get bored.

They need lots of scrambling,

careful brushing

and a good deal of mopping.

Springers don't like ...

having to wait,

being alone,

talking to strangers,

having their ears cleaned,

cats with attitude,

having their fun cut short

or getting into trouble.

Unless it's really fun trouble ...

Springers are ...

quick to learn,

eager to please

and receptive to human emotions ...

well, usually.

They're friendly,

devoted,

trusting,

affectionate,

alert,

intelligent,

always ready for a cuddle,

and always ready to work.

Springers have ...

loving eyes,

flapping ears,

waggy tails,

a great sense of rhythm,

but no sense of style.

They have a distinctive smell,

a penchant for washing,

dribbly mouths,

waxy ears,

and willing hearts.

Springers will ...

never stop running

and never stop fetching.

They'll do anything to please you

just for a cuddle.

They'll make everything a game,

lower your standards,

raise your spirits,

never ignore a puddle,

leave a mark on your clothes ...

and their mark on your heart.

They'll pester you for a walk

and love you for a lifetime.

About the
Illustrator

Jenny MacKendrick studied drawing and applied arts at the University of the West of England. She now works as an artist and illustrator from her studio in Bristol, which she shares with Shona, her large and hairy Hungarian Wirehaired Vizsla, who is often to be found hiding under the desk.

Also in this Series
Labradors
Border Terriers
Pugs